Armory and Lineages of Canada
by
Herbert George Todd

A facsimile copy produced and privately printed by
The Armorial Register Limited
2016

First Published in 2016
by
The Armorial Register Limited
All rights reserved

ISBN: 978-0-9568157-9-8

British Library Cataloguing-in-Publication Data
A catalogue record of this book is available on request from the
British Library

Cover image: The arms of the Province of New Brunswick
(including supporters)

ARMORY AND LINEAGES OF CANADA

ARMORY AND LINEAGES

OF

CANADA

———

Comprising the Lineage of Prominent and Pioneer Canadians
with Descriptions and Illustrations of their Coat
Armor, Orders of Knighthood, or
other Official Insignia.

BY

HERBERT GEORGE TODD

———

HERBERT GEORGE TODD, Editor
39 EAST 42nd STREET
NEW YORK

FROM THE PRESS OF THE NYVALL PRINT, 1876 BROADWAY, NEW YORK

PREFACE

THE purpose of this work is to give a short sketch of the lineage of prominent persons in Canada to-day, with notes of anything of interest or importance regarding any ancestor, and especially to record, briefly but permanently, the achievements of those who, having served their country with distinction, have passed away, but whose names should not be dropped or their deeds forgotten, as is necessarily the case in reference works the scope of which is limited to the living.

It was intended at first to confine the work to families of early settlers; but it cannot be overlooked that Canada, though old in tradition, is yet, in its broad expanse, but a new country, whose citizenship is constantly being augmented by new comers from the older stock of the mother lands. The scope of the work, therefore, will include those who, however recent, are intentionally residents in Canada.

The work will portray the armorials of such of the families herein embraced as have coat-armour and are accustomed to use it, for the recognition and preservation of those cognizances borne by our forefathers tend to enhance the interest and value of family history.

The Heraldic Addenda contain the arms of notables connected with the events in Acadia, New France, and the two Canadas. Others will be added in subsequent sections.

The Provincial Armorials are in accordance with the designs and official descriptions furnished through the kindness of the several Secretaries of the Provinces.

It will be noticed that the shield armorials of the Dominion seem complicated (although composed only of the arms of the first four provinces to enter Confederation), yet are quite bare of those component parts which go to a complete achievement; i. e., crest, supporters, and motto. It is to be hoped that a shield will soon be adopted simpler to the eye, yet more comprehensively representative and having its proper complements.

The Editor is very much indebted to the advice and kind co-operation of the author of "Ontarian Families,"—Mr. E.M. Chadwick, K. C. of Toronto—to whose judgment and learning, especially in ecclesiastical heraldry, the writer has been glad to defer.

HERBERT GEORGE TODD

PUBLISHER'S NOTE.

THOSE who may be interested in honouring their forbears by recording briefly their lineage and acts, or who thus wish to preserve family facts for a generation yet too young to appreciate such matters, are invited to subscribe without delay. Additions to this work are continually in preparation and will be printed and forwarded to all subscribers as soon as sufficient material for a new section is collected. New subscribers will receive all sections issued to date, bound in one volume. Earlier subscribers will be sent the added sections, unbound or bound, as preferred, at cost. Illustrations of the subscribers' paternal or maternal arms and of his wife's family, will be given if furnished.

Additional copies of this book may be had by subscribers for presentation purposes at the rate of 25 cents per section. Minimum price: $1.75 post-paid.

Contents

REFERENCE MARKS

*   See—Morgan's "Canadian Men and Women
        of the Time."

†   "   Burke's "Peerage, Baronetage, Knight-
        age, and Companionage."

‡   "   Chadwick's "Ontarian Families."

§   "   Burke's "General Armory."

Royal Crown

QUARTERLY: 1st and 4th gules, three lions passant-guardant in pale or, for England; 2nd, or, a lion rampant within a double tressure flory-counter-flory gules, for Scotland; 3rd azure, a harp or stringed argent for Ireland: the whole encircled with the garter of blue with gold border bearing the motto in gold "Honi soit qui mal y pense." Crest: Upon the royal helmet, the royal crown proper thereon a lion statent-guardant or, crowned also proper. Supporters: Dexter, a lion guardant or, crowned as in the crest; sinister, a unicorn argent armed, crined, and unguled or, gorged with a cornet composed of crosses patee and fleur-de-lis, a chain affixed thereto, passing between the forelegs and reflected over the back, of the last. Motto (below the shield): "Dieu et mon droit."

Arms of H. R. H. The Duke of Connaught and of Strathearn

The Royal arms differenced by a label of three points argent the center point charged with St. George's Cross, the remaining points each with a fleur-de-lis-azure. In the center of the arms an escutcheon of the arms of Saxony, viz., barry of ten, or and sable, a crown of rue in bend verted. Crest: The Royal crest, excepting that the crowns are replaced by coronets of crosses patee and fleur-de-lis; a label as in the arms. Supporters: The Royal supporters, charged with labels, and the lion having a coronet, as in the crest. No motto. Surrounding the Arms, the Collar with the Garter and the badge pendant therefrom.

ib. R. ib. the Duke of Connaught and Strathearn

H. R. H. Prince ARTHUR WILLIAM PATRICK ALBERT, Duke Connaught and of Strathearn, K. G., K. T., K. P., G. C. B., G. C. S. I., G. C. M. G., G. C. I. E., G. C. V. O., etc.
Born May 1, 1850.
Married 13 March, 1879, H. R. H. Princess Louise Margaret Alexandra Victoria Agnes of Prussia born (1860) and has issue:

> 1. H. R.H. Prince Arthur Frederick Patrick Albert. Born 1883.
> 1. H. R. H. Princess Margaret Victoria Augusta Charlotte Norah (born 1882). Married to H. R. H. Prince Gustavus Adolphus of Sweden.
> 2. H. R. H. Princess Victoria Patricia Helena Elizabeth. Born 1886.

Lineage

ARTHUR of Connaught, born 1850, 3rd Son of
Queen Victoria (and Albert, Prince Consort), daughter of
Edward, Duke of Kent, who died in 1820 (and Victoria of Saxe-Coburg), son of
George III, who died in 1820 (and Sophia Charlotte of Mecklenburg), son of

8

Fredrick Lewis, Prince of Wales, who died in 1751 (and Augusta of Saxe-Gotha), son of

George II, who died in 1760 (and Wilhelmina Caroline of Brandenburg-Anspach), son of

George I, who died in 1727 (and Sophia Dorothea of Zelle), son of

Ernest Augustus, Elector of Hanover, and Sophia, who died in 1714, daughter of

Fredrick V, King of Bohemia, and Elizabeth, daughter of

James I of England, who died in 1625 (and Anne of Denmark), son of

Mary, Queen of Scots (and Henry Stuart, Lord Darnley), daughter of

James V of Scotland (and Mary of Guise), son of

James IV and Margaret, daughter of

Henry VII of England, who died in 1509, and Elizabeth, daughter of

Edward IV of England, who died in 1483 (and Elizabeth Wydeville), son of

Richard, Duke of York (and Lady Cicely Nevill), son of

Richard Plantagenet, Earl of Cambridge, and Lady Ann Mortimer, daughter of

Roger, 4th Earl on March (and Lady Alianore Holland), son of

Edmond, 3rd Earl of March, and Lady Philippa Plantagenet, daughter of

Lionel of Antwerp, Duke of Clarence (and Lady Elizabeth of Ulster), son of

Edward III of England, who died in 1377 (and Philippa of Hainault), son of

Edward II, who died in 1327 (and Isabel of France), son of

Edward I, who died in 1307 (and Eleanor of Castile), son of

Henry III, who died in 1272 (and Eleanor of Provence), son of

John of England, who died in 1216 (and Isabel of Angouleme), son of

Henry II, who died in 1189 (and Eleanor of Aquitaine), son of

Queen Maud of England (and Geoffrey of Anjou), daughter of

Henry I, who died in 1135 (and Matilda of Scotland), son of

William I (the Conqueror, who died in 1087) and Matilda of Flanders.

Baron Strathcona and Mount Royal

SIR DONALD, ALEXANDER SMITH, G. C. M. G., G. C. V. O., F. R. S. * †. Born Forres, Morayshire, Scotland, Aug. 6, 1820. Son of Alexander Smith of Archieston, and Barbara, daughter of Donald Stuart of Leanchoil, Scotland. Came to Canada 1838, entering the Hudson Bay's Co. as a cadet, promoted gradually to be resident governor and Chief Commissioner; appointed by the Dominion Government 1869 to investigate the Red River Insurrection; received thanks of Governor General in Council; M. M. P., Winnipeg, 1870; M. P., Selkirk, 1870; M. P., Montreal West, 1887; appointed, 1896, High Commissioner for Canada

in London. Was considered the most effective promoter of the C. P. R.
Made K. C. M. G. 1886; G. C. M. G. and Member of Privy Council
1896. Raised to Peerage with above title 1897; G. C. V. C. and
F. R. S. 1908; Knight of Grace of St. John of Jerusalem, in England, 1910,
for loyalty, especially for his equipment and maintenance of the "Strathcona
Horse" in the Boer War; Vice-President Bank of Montreal, 1882; President 1887; Honorary Lt. Col. Victoria Rifles, Montreal; Honorary Col.
8th. V. B. King's Liverpool Reg., 15th Light Horse, and 79th. High-
landers; received freedom of the cities of Aberdeen, Edinburgh, Bristol, and
Bath. Was host of Prince and Princess of Wales, Montreal, 1901;
Canadian representative at funeral of Edward VII and at Coronation of
George V. Author of "Western Canada before and since Confederation"
(1897); "The History of the Hudson's Bay Co."(1899). Received honorary degrees from Cambridge, Yale, Aberdeen, Laval, Toronto, Queens,
Ottawa, Durham, and St. Andrews.

Married Isabella Sophia, daughter of Richard Hardisty of the H. B.
C. and has issue:

Margaret Charlotte, heir presumptive to the barony, married Robert
Jared Bliss Howard, M. D., of London, England.

Societies: Royal Colonial Institute; Montreal Nat. Hist. Soc. Brit.

Todd of Ottawa

TODD, ALPHEUS, C. M. C.; L. L. D. (†) (deceased),
Librarian of Parliamentary Library, Ottawa. Born in London,
England, 30 July, 1821. Came to Canada with parents when eleven
years old. In 1834 at the age of thirteen he drew and published the first
map of Toronto, then York. When fifteen years of age (1836) he entered
the public service as Assistant to the Librarian of the Upper Canada Legis-
lature at Toronto. Promoted to the full charge of the Parliamentary Library in 1856. Made Honorary Doctor of Laws by Queen's University
1881, and the same year C. M. G. Author of the following works:
"Practice and Privileges of the Two Houses of Parliament" (1840),
"Parliamentary Government in England" (1866-9), "Parliamentary
Government in the Colonies" (1880). As a Constitutional authority,
acknowledged throughout the British Empire, covering a long period of
his life, and up to the time of his death, he was much consulted in and
outside of Canada by Governors and Ministers, for his opinion on legislative
difficulties, as they arose, in the different Colonies. To this fact the Parliamentary papers of Australasia amply testify.

Married Orillia, Ontario, 1845, Sarah Ann, 2nd daughter and co-heir
of Capt. St. Andrew St. John (q. v.), of his Majesty's 4th and 9th

11

Foot (and great grandson of John, Tenth Baron St. John of Bletshoe in the Peerage of England). Died in Ottawa 1884 and left issue:

1. Philip (1850-99), born, Toronto, wine merchant, married, Seaforth, Ont., June 1, 1881, Rosamond, daughter of Dr. Hiram and Harriet Marie (Smyth) Lee of London, Ont. Died 1899. Issue:

    1. Harriet Eleanor Marguerite, born 1883.

    2. Alpheus Beauchamp, born 1886.

2. Alfred Hamlyn (q. v.).

3. Maude St. John, born, Quebec, 1854, married, Toronto, 1888, John Frederick Hill, commercial traveler (of Mexico, Mo.), son of John and Eleanor (Buckner) Hill of London, England. Issue:

    Eleanor Maude, born 1890.

4. Ernest William, born, Toronto, 1858, R. N. W. Mounted Police; Later Agent B. & O. R. R., Baltimore, Md. Married, Auburn, New York, 1899, Lillian, daughter of William Edwin Kemp, of Colborne, Ont. Issue:

    1. Alpheus Cameron, born 1899.

    2. Maude St. John, born 1900.

5. Herbert George, born, Quebec, 1863, Mechanical engineer, Buenos Ayres & Rosario R. R., Campana, Argentine Republic; Railroad Agent N. Y. C. R. R. and Artist, Yonkers, New York. Married, Campana, May 24th, 1891, Marcella Marguerita, daughter of Michael and Winnifred (Mannion) Murtagh of Giles, Prov. de Buenos Ayres. Issue:

    Juanita Guellermina, born April 4th, 1892.

Lineage

Samuel Todd (1752-1820), married (Stepney, London, England) Mary Randall of Shorditch, London; died Stepney. Issue:

    1. Robert (had two daughters, one son, all died unmarried).

    2. Henry Alpheus Randall Cook (below).

    3. William, died Toronto, leaving several children.

Henry Alpheus Randall Cook (1782-1861) (Oxon) Book-dealer and amateur artist of ability, married Mary Ann (daughter of William Pointz Patrick [vide Patrick] and Mary Randall of Needham Market, Suffolk). Came to Canada 1832; author "Notes upon Canada and the United States" (1840). Died Toronto. Issue:

    1. Alfred, born Halstead, Essex, 1819 (q. v.).

    2. Alpheus (as above).

Arms: Sable, two bars wavy between three martlets or: on a shield of pretence, argent, on a chief gules, two mullets or, (for St. John). Crest: A wolf's head or, collared flory-counter-flory gules. Pendent from the escutcheon, the badge of a Companion of the Most Distinguished Order of St. Michael and St. George.

Grant of Ottawa.

SIR JAMES ALEXANDER GRANT, K. C. M. G (* †), M. D. McGill 1854; F. R. C. S., Edinburgh, 1860; M. R. C. S., London 1860; F. R. C. P., London 1873; fifteen years in Parliament for Russel county and for Ottawa; in 1872 introduced a bill to construct the Canadian Pacific Ry.; President and Chief of Staff of the General Hospital for twenty-five years; Physician to the Governors-General of Canada since 1865; Ex-President Ontario Medical Council; President Literary and Scientific Soc.; President Ottawa Art Assn.; Vice-President International Medical Congress, Washington, D. C.; Hon. President Public Health Assn. of Canada; Hon. President University of Edinburgh Club of North America; Hon. Member American Academy of Medicine; Hon. Member British Medical Assn; holds Medal from "del Benemeriti Italiani" of Palermo; member, Legion of Honor of Italy, 1887; Knighted 1887.

Sir James was born Aug. 11, 1831, Inverness, Scotland; married Ottawa, 1856, Maria (daughter of Edward Malloch, M. P. for Carleton, merchant of Richmond, Ont., and Margaret Hill). Issue:

1. Lt. Col. James Alexander, M. D., P. M. O., of **Toronto**.
2. Henry Young, M. D., of Niagara Falls, Ont.
3. Jessie, married George R. Major, of Niagara Falls, **Ont.**

4. Mary Louise, married James Arthur Cochrane of Hillhurst, P. Q.   She died 1890.

5. Edward Cruickshanks, lumber merchant.

6. William Wright, electrical engineer.

7. Gwenn.

8. Harriot.

Club: Rideau.   Residence: The Roxburg, Laurier Ave., Ottawa.

Lineage.

James Grant, born at and resident of Corrimony Co., Inverness, Scotland, a barrister; was awarded in 1819 a prize by the Highland Society of all Scotland, for the best history of the Gaelic language, and other historical papers; his son

James (1820-82), born Inverness, a physician of Edinburgh, married Jane Ogilvy of Inverness; issue: three sons and six daughters; of these sons, James Alexander (above) is one.

Arms: Gules three antique crowns or, within a bordure checky of the second and first. Crest: A demi-savage proper.   Motto: "I'll stand sure."   The shield is surrounded by the circlet with pendant badge of the Most Distinguished Order of St. Michae and St. George.

Viscount Monck.

THE appointment of Lord Monck in 1861 to the office of Captain General and Governor in Chief of Canada was not favorably received by the Canadian press at the time, on the ground that he "was an inexperienced and unknown man, utterly unpracticed in any kind of statesmanlike work" to guide the Ship of State at the critical period of approaching Confederation. He was not long in office, however, when stirring events proved that he possessed all the ability necessary to meet the occasion. First came 'The Trent affair," 1862, that raised bad blood in the country, and required wise and tactful administration. Then in 1864 a Ministerial crisis was brought about through parties being too evenly balanced in the House and the Government was defeated by two on a measure of vital importance to the country. On petition of the Ministry for dissolution, His Excellency, while expressing his willingness to abide by the advice of his ministers, set forth, in an able memorandum, the difficulties of the situation and advised a course that would avoid appealing to the electorate, where there seemed, through the excited condition of the country, but little chance of a satisfactory result. The wisdom of this advice the Ministry acknowledged and followed. Under his regime the plan of Confederation was worked out and accomplished in 1867, he becoming first Governor General; he relinquished office in 1868. (A. Hamlyn Todd.)

Arms: Gules, a chevron between three lions' heads, erased argent. Crest: A wyvern, wings, addorsed, sable. Supporters: Dexter, a wyvern wings addorsed, argent langued gules, holding over the dexter shoulder a laurel branch fructed proper; sinister, a lion argent langued gules holding over the sinister shoulder a laurel branch fructed proper. Motto: "Fortiter, fideliter, feliciter." Over the shield the coronet of a viscount and, surrounding the shield, the collar, and circlet, with pendant badge of a Knight Grand Cross of S. Michael and St. George.

Chadwick of Toronto.

EDWARD MARION CHADWICK (* ‡), of Toronto; Barrister at law (since 1863), K. C.; Major retired from 2nd Regt. the Queen's Own Rifles; Lay Canon and Treasurer of St Albans' Cathedral, Toronto; an Honorary Chief of the Six Nations Indians, having been adopted by Chiefs in Council into the Anowara, or Turtle Clan of the Mohawk Nation, by the name of Shagotyohgwisaks. Born 22 Sept., 1840, third son of John Craven Chadwick, who came to Canada in 1837 and settled in the Township of Ancaster, afterwards Guelph, and his wife Louisa, daughter of Jonathan Bell (see Foster's Royal Descents), who was fourth son of John Craven Chadwick of Ballinard, Tipperary, Ireland. Is member of the Convention International d'Heraldique (European Continental), and of the Society of Genealogists of London, England. Author of "Ontarian Families."

Married (firstly) 28 June, 1864, Ellen Byrne, daughter of James Beatty of Toronto, who died 10 Feb., 1865; married (secondly) 20 Feb., 1868, Maria Martha, daughter of Alexander Fisher, and has had issue. See following article.

Residence: "Lanmar," 107 Howland Ave., Toronto.

Arms: Per pale gules and sable; within an orle of eight martlets argent an inescutcheon of the same charged with a cross gules, in the first quarter a crescent sable: with an escutcheon of pretence (for Fisher) azure, three fishes argent naiant in pale, on a chief or a kingfisher proper between two fraises gules. Crest: A white martlet bearing in his bill a white lily stemmed and leaved proper borne fesseways the flowers to the sinister. Mottoes: Above, "In candore decus;" beneath, "Toujours pret."

The sons and daughters of the foregoing are:

1. William Craven Vaux Chadwick, of Toronto, architect; Lieut. Col. commanding 9th Mississauga Horse, Active Militia of Canada. Born, 6 Dec., 1868, married Jessie Dorothea, daughter of Robert Murray, merchant in New York (descendant of an officer of the Garrison of Londonderry, Ireland, during the seige in 1688), had issue Patricia Katherine, who died in infancy.

2. Edward Alister Eade, of the Imperial Bank, Toronto. Born 13 Feb , 1871, married Florence Edith, daughter of Capt. Thomas Campbell Kemp, and has issue:
    1. Edward Norman Loud.
    2. Austin Ralph.
    3. Florence Marion (by official registration in Montreal John Marion).

3. George D'Arcy Austin, of the Manufacturers' Life Insurance Co. Artist; born 22 Feb., 1880, married Bessie Carlisle, daughter of Capt. John Edward Mac Corqudale.

4. Richard Ellard Carden, of Montreal, Civil Engineer. Born, Feb. 16, 1885.

5. Bryan Damer Seymour, of Toronto, architect; born 24 June, 1888.

1. Fanny Marion, married to James Grayson Smith, of Toronto, barrister at law, and died, leaving issue :
    Hugh Henderson Grayson Smith.

2. Louisa Mary Caroline.

Arms: Quarterly: 1 and 4 (same as above, without escutcheon of pretence). 2 and 3 (same as above, escutcheon of pretence). Crest: (same as above) with motto, "In candore decus." 2. A lion rampant azure, holding a maple leaf gules with motto, "Hope wins success." Motto, beneath, "Toujours pret."

Cockshutt of Brantford.

WILLIAM FOSTER COCKSHUTT (*), M. P., born Brantford Ont., 17 Oct., 1855. Member for Brantford 1904-8, and 1911; merchant; manufacturer; Ex-president, Cockshutt Plow Co., Member Electric Power Commission of Ontario; six times delegate to the Chamber of Commerce of the Empire; fifteen years member Council of Toronto Board of Trade, on directorate of several companies. Chairman, Laycock Orphanage; Member Executive Synod of Huron, and of General Synod.

He married Brantford, April 8, 1891, Minnie Turner, daughter of the Rev. Robert Ashton (and Alice Turner of London, England), principal of the Mohawk Institute of Brantford. Issue:

1. William Ashton, born July 28, 1892.
2. George Turner, born Feb. 17, 1894.
3. Eric Morton, born Jan. 23, 1896.
4. Maude Leslie, born July 4, 1898.
5. Clarence Foster, born July 16, 1901.
6. Phyllis Ashton, born June 7, 1903.

Residences: Brantford, Ont.   Lake of Bays (Muskoka, Ont).

Clubs: Brantford Club; Country Club; Dufferin Rifle Mess; National. (Toronto).

Lineage.

Edmund Cockshutt, a wealthy manufacturer and farm-owner of Worsaw Hill, Clitheroe, Lancashire, had a grandson

James Cockshutt, a manufacturer of Bradford York, and Colne Lanc. (firm of J. & J. Cockshutt). Married, 1810, Mary Nightingale, a cousin of the celebrated Florence Nightingale and daughter-in-law of Benjamin Ingham, founder of that sect.   Came to Canada 1827 in bark "Lady Digby" for Quebec; thence by stage to York, U. C. Established business there and later at Brantford (subsequently the I. & J. Cockshutt Co.). In 1840 re-visited England to pay off all business debts contracted through his failure in the cotton famine, previous to emigrating. Died Toronto 1866. Issue:

1. Jane, married Alfred Laycock of Blenheim, Ont.
2. Ignatius, born Bradford, York, 1812, a gentleman of sterling worth and integrity; a pioneer, manufacturer, promoter, and philanthropist, known in later years as "the grand old man of Brantford," connected with the following enterprises: The Grand River Nav. Co.; Director of the Buffalo, Goderich & Lake Huron R. R. (first railway through Brantford); President of the B. Gas Co., The B. Water Works, the Craven Cotton Co.; Vice-President of the Cockshutt Plow Co. Built the B. Orphans' Home. He married (firstly) Montreal, 1846, Margaret, daughter of Alexander Gemmel (of Paisley, Scotland, and of Montreal). She died 1847, leaving issue:

Mary M., married to George Kippan of Brantford.

Married (secondly) 1850, Elizabeth (daughter of Francis Foster of Subden, Lanc.). She died 1891. He died Brantford 1901. Issue:

    1. James, born 1852.
    2. Charles.
    3. William Foster (as above).
    4. Frank.
    5. Alice (died young).
    6. Edward L.
    7. Elizabeth, married George Drummond, of Montreal.
    8. Helen R.
    9. Henry (president of the Cockshutt Plow Co.).

Arms: Gules guttee argent on a chief or a griffin passant sable. Crest: A demi-griffin sable.

Buchanan of Montreal.

A RTHUR WILLIAM PATRICK BUCHANAN, K. C. (*), born Montreal, 4th Nov., 1870, Advocate and King's Counsel; author of "The Buchanan Book."

Married, Stoke Poges, Bucks, England, June 2, 1897, Berthe Louise, daughter of William Quirin, merchant of Boston, Mass. (and Isabelle Mercer). Issue:

1. Erskine Brock Quirin, born 1898.
2. Audrey Isabel Patricia, born 1900.

Clubs: St. James, Montreal Hunt, Royal Montreal Golf. Societies: The Buchanan, The Champlain. Residence: 731 Pine Ave. West, Montreal.

Lineage.

Alexander Buchanan (1706-1810), born near Fintona, resident or Ednasop or Milltown Co., Tyrone, Ireland, died Ednasop (descended from William Buchanan, the last Laird of Blairvockie, who sold that estate about 1695 and went to Ireland); his son

Dr. John Buchanan (1769-1815), born Eccles Green, near Fintona, Army Surgeon H. M. 49th. Foot; married (firstly) Lucy Richardson, who died 1803. Issue:

    1. Alexander (below).
    2. John (1800-37), married Catherine Grant.
    3. Jane Mary (1801-72), married William Hall.

Married (secondly) Ursule (daughter of Hon. Joseph Francois Perrault of Quebec), died Quebec. His son

Alexander Buchanan (1798-1851), Q. C., born Gosport, England. Admitted to Bar of Lower Canada 1819; Kings Counsel 1835; Commissioner for L. C. in settlement of boundaries between the Canadas; Judge of the Court of Requests 1839; Crown Prosecutor, 1840-5; Member of Council, Montreal Bar 1851. (For fuller information see the Buchanan Book.) Married Mary Ann, daughter of James Buchanan (1772-1851); British Consul at New York 1816-43; died Montreal. Issue:

    1. George Carlo Vidua (1825-1901), Judge of the Superior Court of the District of Bedford. Married Abbie Louisa Snow. (Issue.)
    2. Elizabeth Jane (1827-97), married Lt. Col. George Blicke Champion de Crespigny, son of Charles Fox de Crespigny of Uxbridge, Middlesex. (Issue.)
    3. Wentworth James (1828-1905), married Agatha, daughter of Major Arnold R. Burrowes, 3rd Foot Guards, and later of Woodstock U. C. (Issue.)
    4. William Robert (1830-1902), married (firstly) Miss Muslewhite, married (secondly) Emma Brickwood. (Issue.)
    5. Alexander Brock (below).
    6. Margaret Lucy (1834-7).
    7. Frederick Albert (1836-42).
    8. Mary Alexandrina (1841-died young).
    9. Mary (1842-1901), married Rev. R. Mainwaring Williams of Harnhill Rectory, Cirencester, Gloucestershire. (Issue.)

Alexander Brock Buchanan (above), born Montreal 1832; banker; married Elizabeth Ann, daughter of Francis Best of Montreal. Issue:

    1. George Reid (1858-61).
    2. Alexander, born 1861, married Anne Mary, daughter of Hon. James O'Brien of Montreal.
    3. Robert Charles, born 1867, married Mary Jane, daughter of William McLimont of Quebec. (Issue.)
    4. Arthur William Patrick (as above).
    5. Albert Edward Clarence (twin), born 1870.

1. Elizabeth Emily (1859-80).
2. Frances (Lily), married Arthur H. Buchanan of Spokane, Wash.
3. Ethel (Cherry) (1865-98).
4. Gwendoline (1877-96).

Arms: Or, a lion rampant sable within a double tressure, flory-counter-flory gules. Crest: A hand holding up a ducal cap, purple, lined ermine, tufted on the top with a rose gules, within two branches of laurel disposed orleways proper. Motto: "Juvo Audaces."

Cassels of Ottawa.

WALTER GIBSON PRINGLE CASSELS (* ‡), born Quebec, 14 August, 1845; Judge of the Exchequer Court of Canada, appointed 2 March, 1908; Q. C., 1883.

Married Quebec, Sept. 24, 1873, Susan, daughter of Robert Hamilton of Hamwood, Quebec (see Hamilton of Hamwood), and Isabella Thomson. Issue:

1. Isabel Hamilton (1875-86).
2. Robert Cecil Hamilton, born August 2, 1876, married, Oct. 25, 1905, Mollie Waldie, daughter of John Waldie of Toronto. (Issue.)
3. Mary Kathleen Hamilton, born April 5, 1878; married, Toronto, Feb. 22, 1905, Harry Duncan Lockart Gordon, of Toronto. (Issue.)
4. Harriet Frances Hamilton, born Jan. 1, 1880.

5. George Hamilton, born July 17, 1882, married, Toronto, Sept. 30, 1909, Cecil Vivian Kerr, daughter of Hon. James Kirkpatrick Kerr (q. v.) of Toronto.
6. Susie Hamilton, born Jan. 19, 1884.
7. Walter Craigie Hamilton (1887-92).
8. Jessie Hamilton, born May 15, 1890.

Clubs: Toronto, and Toronto Golf; Rideau, and Country Club (Ottawa); Halifax Club.

Residence: 21 Blackburn Ave., Ottawa.

Lineage.

Walter Gibson Pringle Cassels (as above), son of

Major Robert Cassels (1815-82), born Leith, Scotland; bank manager, Evesham, Worcestershire; came to Canada 1837; manager British Bank of North America, Quebec, 1841; Montreal, 1855; President St. Andrews Soc., Quebec and Toronto; President St. James Club, Montreal; Director G. T. R.; Trustee Queen's College, Kingston; Major, Montreal Volunteer Artillery; married 1838, Halifax, Mary Gibbens (daughter of Hon. Jas. Mac Nab, Receiver General of Nova Scotia); his father

Walter Gibson Cassels (1777-1868), born Leith; inherited estate of his maternal grandfather Walter Gibson(see below); Manager National Bank of Scotland; a noted author on currency questions; consulted by Parliament; Chief Magistrate, Leith 1813; married, Janet (daughter of John Scugall, merchant of Leith); died a strong Christian; his father

Andrew Cassels (1731-1814), born Barrowstowness (Bo'ness), Chief Magistrate, Leith 1800; a wealthy shipowner and merchant; a religious, amiable and hospitable man; married (firstly) Margaret, daughter of John Ritchie (seven generations of John Ritchies were born and died in the same house at Bo'ness); married (secondly) Anne (daughter of Walter Gibson of Greenknowe, Stirlingshire, whose Saxon lineage see below); she was mother of Walter Gibson Cassels (above): Andrew was son of

James Cassels (1696-1760), born Bo'ness; merchant shipowner; James was son of

Andrew Cassillis, born Bo'ness 1668; merchant shipowner, and Chief Magistrate; he married Hannah (daughter of John Gib of Bo'ness); his father

James Cassillis, born 1624; a wealthy shipowner of Bo'ness; married Euphemia Cassillis.

Arms (Registered Lyon office 1864): Argent, a chevron gules between two cross crosslets fitchee in chief, and a key fesseways ward downwards in base sable. Crest; A dolphin naiant or. Motto, above the crest: "Avise la fin."

WALTER GIBSON.

Lineage.

Walter Gibson (1717-1800), Laird of Greenknowe, Stirlingshire, Scotland, son of

Dr. John Gibson (1666-1765)and Catherine Home, daughter of

George Home, 4th Laird of Bassendean (and Catherine Pringle); son of

Alexander Home, 3rd Laird (and Sibella Brown); son of

George Home, 2nd Laird (and Jean Seaton); son of

William Home, 1st Laird (and Mariotte Pringle); 3rd son of

Sir John Home, of Coldingknows (and Margaret, daughter of Sir Andrew Kerr of Cessford, ancestor of the Duke of Roxburghe); son of

Mongo Home, of Coldingknows (and Elizabeth, daughter of James, Earl of Buchanan, descendant of King Edward III); son of

John Home, of Whitrigs and Ersilton, ambassador to England 1491; 2nd son of

Alexander, 1st Lord Home (creation 1493); son of

Sir Thomas Home (and Nicola Pepdie, heiresss of Dunglass); son of

Sir John Home; son of

Roger Home; son of

Galfridus Home; son of

William, first to use the surname "Home;" son of

William by his 2nd wife Ada, daughter of Patrick, Earl of Dunbar and March (a descendant of King William the Lyon); son of

William, of Greenlaw; 2nd son of

Gospatrick, 3rd Earl of Dunbar and March; son of

Gospatrick, 2nd Earl of Dunbar and March; son of

Gospatrick, 1st Earl of Dunbar and March; son of

Gospatrick, a Saxon nobleman, and Agablia, who was daughter of Uthred, a Saxon Prince of Northumberland (and Princess Elgiva, daughter of King Ethelred II of England); son of

King Edgar (and Elfrida); son of

King Edmund I; son of

King Edward I; son of

King Alfred, the Great.

Todd of Ottawa.

A LFRED HAMLYN TODD (*), born Toronto, 25 Oct., 1851, son of ALPHEUS TODD (q. v.) of Ottawa, Ont. Entered the Civil Service 1869 as clerk, Library of Parliament, Ottawa. Is now Chief

Clerk. Served in all ranks of the Militia of Canada from cadet (1866) to Lieut.-Col. Governor General's Foot Guards; resigned 1892. Holds 1st. class Military School Certificate, Halifax 1874; Member Wimbledon teams 1879 and 1880, Adjutant Bisley team 1890; Commanded Ottawa Contingent Northwest Rebellion 1885 (medal); V. O. Service Decoration. Edited 2nd editions "Todd's Parliamentary Government in England" (1887); "Parliamentary Government in the Colonies" (1894).

Married Ottawa 1884, Amelia Annie, daughter of John Bell Gordon, of Goderich, Ont., and Elizabeth Amelia MacDonald. Issue:
1. Cyril Gordon, born 16 July, 1885 ; died young.
2. Mona Gertrude, born 16 Jan., 1887; married, 7th. Sept., 1904, Herbert Edward (son of William Flewker and Elizabeth Geldart of Bedford, Eng.) Issue :
    1. Aline (died infant).
    2. Dorothea Leslie.
3. Ambrose St. John, born 1st. May, 1889, died young.
4. Basil Gordon, born 7th. Oct., 1890.
5. Edith St. John, born 5th. Nov., 1894.
6. Oswald Gordon, born 17th. Sept., 1896.
7. Keith Hamlyn, born 5th. Nov., 1898.
8. Gwytha Beryl, born 25th. Feb., 1904.

Residence: 13 Kent St, Ottawa. Club: Rivermead Golf.

Arms:—Quarterly: 1st. and 4th. Sable, two bars wavy between three martlets or, (for Todd): 2nd. and 3rd, argent, on a chief gules, two mullets or, (for St. John) Crest: A wolf's head or, collared flory-counter-flory gules. Motto: "Duris non frangor."

Brymner of Montreal

WILLIAM BRYMNER (*), P. R. C. A., born, Greenock, Scotland, 14th. Dec., 1855; came with his parents to Canada when two years old; artist; unmarried. Studied painting in Paris under William A. Bouguereau and Tony Robert Fleury from 1878-84; in charge of the Art school of the Art Association, Montreal, since 1886; Pres. R. C. A. since 1909; received gold medal for painting, Pan-American Exhibition, Buffalo, N. Y., 1902, and silver medal, St. Louis, Mo., Exhibition 1904.

Clubs: St. James, Pen and Pencil (Montreal). Societies: Royal Canadian Academy of Arts, Canadian Art Club (Toronto). Residence: 255 Bleury St., Montreal.

Lineage

Alexander Brymner, born Sterling, Scotland, a landed proprietor, married Mary Crawford. His son

Alexander, born Sterling, 1755, an army contractor who died at Sterling, leaving issue.

Alexander (1788-1861), born Sterling, a banker at Greenock, married Elizabeth, daughter of John Fairlie. He died at Greenock. His son

Douglas (1823-1902), born Greenock, came to Canada 1857. First Dominion Archivist, Ottawa; L. L. D. Queens; married Jean, daughter of William Thomson of Greenock. Died New Westminister, B. C., while visiting. Issue:

      1. Alexander (1854-5).

      2. William (as above).

      3. George Douglas, born 1857, married Anne Elizabeth Harrison of Stratford, Ont.

      4. Anne Steel (1859-72).

      5. James Greenshields, born 1861, married Rose Armstrong of New Westminster, B. C.

      6. Elizabeth Fairlie, born 1863, married Frederick Colson, Department of the Secretary of State, Ottawa.

      7. Cecil Stuart Graham (1869-76).

      8. Agnes Jean (1871-90).

      9. Robert Thomson, born 1875, married George Grace Stuart of Belleville, Ont.

St. John of Orillia.

ST. JOHN OF ORILLIA

ST. ANDREW ST. JOHN (†) (deceased), born 28 June, 1794,
Captain in H. B. M's. 4th Foot and 9th Foot, married in old Kirk
Bradden, Douglas, Isle-of-Man, Margaret, eldest daughter of Philip Moore,
(q. v.) of "Bal'a Moore," near Peel. Came to Canada and settled on a
grant of land at Orillia, U. C. Died 1838. Issue:

1. Jane Margaret married (firstly) James Scott of Orillia, who
died in 1847; (secondly) 1860, Toronto, Lucius Richard
O'Brien (q. v.,) of Shanty Bay, Ont.

2. Sarah Ann married 1845 Alpheus Todd of Montreal.
(See Todd of Ottawa.)

3. Arabella Diana Hamlyn, married 1849 George Hallen
of Orillia. (She died 1910.)

Lineage.

St. Andrew St. John (above) was eldest son of

Ambrose St. John (1760-1823) and Arabella (daughter of Sir. James Hamlyn, Bart.,
whose wife Arabella was niece and heir of Sir Nicholas Williams, Kt. of
Edwinsford, Carmarthen, Lord Lieutenant of the county, who died Sept. 1745). He
was eldest son of

Very Rev. St. Andrew St. John, D. D., Dean of Worcester, 1732-95 (and Sarah, daughter of Thomas Chase of Bromley Kent), who was second son of

John, 10th Baron St. John (and Elizabeth, daughter of Sir Ambrose Crowley of
Greenwich, Sheriff of London, 1706-7, who obtained a grant of arms §. His
father Ambrose Crowley, a Quaker of Stourbridge at the Visitations of 1682-3,
"disclaimed all right to arms and gentility"). He died 1757. He was fourth son of

Sir Andrew St. John, 2nd Bart. (and Jane, only daughter of Sir William Blois § of
Cockfield Hall, Suffolk). He died 1701. He was eldest son of

Sir Oliver St. John, created baronet 1601 (died 1661) and Barbara, daughter and co-heir
of John St. Andrew § of Gotham, Notts. (a descendant of Paganus de St. Andrew
temps, Henry II, Visitation of Notts, 1614). His father

Sir Roland St. John, K. B., M. P., for Bedfordshire, married Sybilla, daughter of John
Vaughan of Hargast Hereford, and died 1645; was fourth son of

Oliver, 3rd Baron St. John (whose eldest son Oliver was 1st. Earl of Bolingbroke). He
married Dorothy (daughter of Sir John Rede of Odington, Co. Gloucester). He
died 1618; was second son of

26

Oliver, elevated to the Peerage 1558, as 1st Lord St. John of Bletshoe, who sat in judgment (*temps* Elizabeth) upon Thomas, Duke of Norfolk. He married Agnes (daughter of John Fisher and granddaughter and heir of Sir Michael Fisher, Knt.). He died 1582. His father

Sir John St. John married Margaret (daughter of Sir William Waldegrave, K. B., of Smallbridge, Suffolk). [Arms per pale argent and gules.] He was eldest son of

Sir John St. John, K. B., of Bletshoe (and Sybl, daughter of Morgan ap Jenkyns ap Philip), son of

Sir John St. John, K. B. (and Alice, daughter of Sir Thomas Bradshaigh ⁂ of Haig, Co. Lancaster, a descendant of Sir John Bradshaw, a Saxon living at the Conquest), eldest son of

Sir Oliver St. John of Bletshoe and Penmark, who married (*temps* Henry VI) Margaret (daughter of Sir John, Lord Beauchamp, and sister and heir of John, Lord Beauchamp, ⁂ of Bletshoe [title created 1363]. Note: After Sir Oliver died; Margaret married, secondly, 1440, John Beaufort, Duke of Somerset, and their only child Margaret married, 1455, Edmund Tudor, Earl of Richmond, who was, by her, father of Henry VII). Sir Oliver was a descendant of

William de St. John of Faumont, Co. Glamorgan, second son of

Robert de St. John, Lord of Basing, Co. Southampton, who was summoned by Henry III "to be at Chester on Monday next after the Feast of St. John the Baptist well accoutered with horse and arms to oppose the incursions of the Welsh." He married Agnes, daughter of William de Cantelupe ⁂. His father

William de St. John, who assumed the name of his maternal ancestors, was son of

Mabil Orvyl (and Adam de Port, a powerful feudal baron of Basing). She was daughter of

Muriel (and Reginald de Aura Valle or Orvyl), a daughter of

Roger de St. John, who married Cicely, daughter and heiress of Robert de Haya, lord of the Manor of Halnac, Suffolk, a kinsman of Henry I. Roger's father

John de St. John of Stanton, Oxfordshire, a man of great eminence in the reign of William Rufus, was one of twelve knights who accompanied the Earl of Gloucester in a war against the Welsh and received, "in reward for his great services and helps and many victories," the castle of Faumont, Glamorgan. His father

William de St. John (whose name came from the territory of St. John, near Rouen) came into England with William the Conqueror as grand master of artillery and supervisor of the wagons and carriages, whence the horses' hames or collars were born as his cognizance (Burke). He married Olivia, daughter of Ralph de Filgiers of Normandy.

Arms (Quartering Beauchamp and St. Andrew): Argent on a chief gules two mullets or. Crest: On a mount vert a falcon rising or, belled of the last, ducally gorged gules. Motto: "Data fata secutus." Note: J. H. Round in his English "Libro d'Oro" says that St. John is the only peerage family descended in the male line from an ancestor living in the time of Doomsday.

Fleming of Ottawa

SIR SANFORD FLEMING, K. C. M. G., L. L. D., M. I. C. E., etc. (* † §), son of ANDREW GREIG FLEMING and ELIZABETH ARNOT. Born Kirkaldy, Fifeshire, Scotland, 1827, where he was educated as a surveyor and engineer. Emigrated 1845, entering service of the Northern R. R. of Canada, becoming chief engineer in 1857. Was sent 1863 to England, to promote railroad communication between the Red River District (now Manitoba) and the East; was chief engineer during construction of the Intercolonial R. R.; largely responsible for the successful construction of the C. P. R.; responsible for the establishing of universal time; planned the construction of the British Empire chain of cables. Author of many books covering his several projects in Dominion and Empire affairs. Member of many geographical societies; Vice-President of the United Empire League.

Married, 1855, Ann Jean, daughter of the late Sheriff Hall of Peterboro, Ont.

Residence: "Winterholme," Ottawa.

(For a fuller account of the life of this most loyal, eminent, and remarkable man see Morgan's "Canadian Men and Women of the Time"-- 1912.)

Arms: Gules a chevron within a double tressure flory-counter-flory argent. Crest: A goat's head erased argent armed or. Motto: "Let the deed shaw." Surrounding the shield, the circlet and pendant badge of a Knight Commander of the Most Distinguished Order of St. Michael and St. George.

Ibamilton of Ibamwood (Quebec).

JOHN HAMILTON, ESQ. (* §), M. A., D. C. L., Chancellor University of Bishop's College, Lennoxville, Quebec. Retired merchant. Born 7 Sept., 1851, New Liverpool, Quebec. Married 25 April, 1877, at Quebec, Ida Mary, daughter of Alexander Carlisle Buchanan (and C. L. C. Bowen, his wife), Immigration Commissioner at Quebec. Issue:

> 1. Constance Naomi, born 1879; married, 1905, Arthur Carington Smith.
> 2. Edith Craigie, born 1881.
> 3. Mary Frances Vera, born 1885.
> 4. Jessie Irene, born 1887.

Clubs: Quebec Garrison, Royal Canadian Yacht, American Universities (London). Societies: Quebec Literary and Historical Society; Champlain Society (President).

Residences: Hamwood, Quebec. "Moss Craig," Cacouna, Quebec.

Lineage.

Hugh Hamilton, of Ballybreagh, Ireland, married Mary Ross, of Rostrevor. **He died** 1728. Issue:

Alexander Hamilton, M. P., who died 1768. Issue:

Charles Hamilton, who married Elizabeth (daughter of Crewe Chetwood). **He died 1818.** Issue:

George Hamilton, born Sheephill, Co. Meath, Ireland; came to Canada 1808, became a lumber merchant at Hawkesbury, Ont.; married Susanna C. (daughter of John Craigie); died 1839, Hawkesbury. Issue:

    1. Robert (1822-98).

    2. George (1824-56).

    3. John (1827-88), Senator.

    4. Charles, born 1834, Archbishop of Ottawa (q. v.).

    5. Francis, born 1838.

Robert Hamilton (1822-98), born New Liverpool, Quebec; a lumber merchant of Quebec; and Hawkesbury; married Isabella H. (daughter of John Thomson of Quebec) died Quebec. Issue:

    1. Isabella, born 1845, married Col. De La C. T. Irwin, C. M. G. (q. v.).

    2. Susan, born 1847, married Hon. Walter Gibson Pringle Cassels, K. C., Judge of the Exchequer Court (q. v.).

    3. George (1850-80).

    4. John, born 1851 (as above).

    5. Robina, born 1853.

    6. Frances (1855-88).

    7. Jessie (1857-86).

    8. Henrietta M., born 1863, married Archdeacon Cole, D. C. L., B. D. of Taranaki New Zealand.

See "Hamilton of Hamwood" in Burke's "Landed Gentry of Ireland," 1904.

Arms: Quarterly gules and argent; in the first and fourth quarters, three cinquefoils pierced ermine and a canton of the second charged with a trefoil slipped vert: in the second and third quarters a lymphad with the sails furled, and oars out sable. Crest: Out of a ducal coronet or, an oak-tree fructed and penetrated transversely in the main-stem by a frame-saw proper, frame or, the blade bearing the word "Through;" suspended from one of the branches a shield argent charged with a trefoil slipped vert. Motto: "Sola Nobilitas Virtus."

Hamilton of Ottawa.

THE MOST REVEREND CHARLES HAMILTON, D. D., D. C. L., Archbishop (Anglican) of Ottawa and Metropolitan of Canada (* ‡). Born at Hawkesbury, Ont., 6 Jan., 1834. Graduate of University College of Oxford, England; D. D. Bishop's College, Lennoxville; D. C. L. Trinity, Toronto; consecrated a Bishop of the Church of God on the Festival of St. Philip and St. James, May 1st, 1885, and enthroned in the Cathedral in Hamilton, Ont., as Bishop of Niagara; translated to the diocese of Ottawa, and enthroned in the Cathedral as first Bishop of Ottawa, May 1st, 1896; First Archbishop of Ottawa since 1899.

Married 25 Feb., 1862, at St Michael's Church, Quebec,

Frances Louisa Hume, daughter of Tannatt Houston Thomson, Deputy Commissary General of Toronto, and Margaret Anne Ussher. Issue:

1. Charles Robert, born Aug. 15, 1867, of Vancouver.
2. Lilian Margaret, born June 16, 1869.
3. Mabel Frances, born July 25, 1870; married Edward Kirwan Counsell Martin of Hamilton. (Issue.)
4. Ethel Mary, born Nov. 14, 1871.
5. Hubert Valentine (1873-1903).
6. Winnifred Katherine (1875-80).
7. Harold Francis (Rev.), born Oct. 5, 1876, of Bishop's College, Lennoxville.
8. Mary Agnes, born 1878.
9. George Theodore, born July 5, 1881.

Residence: Archbishop's Palace, 495 Wilbrod St., Ottawa

Lineage

Dr. Hamilton is the 4th son of Lt. Col. George Hamilton of Quebec and Hawkesbury, Ont. (and Lucy Susanna Christiana Craigie). [See Hamilton of Hamwood.]

Arms: Party per pale; Dexter, argent a cross gules, in the first quarter a key surmounted by a pastoral staff in saltire proper. On a chief azure an oak tree issuing from a ducal coronet, the trunk pierced by a saw bearing the word "Through," all proper the frame or (for Diocese of Ottawa): Sinister; quarterly, 1st and 4th gules three cinquefoils pierced ermine, a canton argent charged with a trefoil vert; 2nd and 3rd argent a lymphad sable (for Hamilton). Motto: "Sola Nobilitas Virtus." Over the shield the mitre of a Bishop. Note: The tree in the diocesan arms is taken, in compliment to Dr. Hamilton as first bishop, from his family crest. Burke gives the following account of the origin of this crest: "Sir Gilbert Hamilton, founder of the family, having slain John de Spencer in a rencounter, fled from the court of Edward II. Being pursued, he and his attendant changed clothes with two wood-cutters, and, taking their saws, were in the act of cutting through an oak tree, when his pursuers passed by. Perceiving his servant notice them, Sir Gilbert hastily called out: 'Through,' which word, with the oak and saw through it, he took for a crest to commemorate his deliverance."

Irwin of Ottawa.

COL. DE LA CHEROIS THOMAS IRWIN, C. M. G. (* †), Hon. A. D. C. to the Earl of Minto and to Earl Grey, Governors-General; born Carnagh House, Co. Armagh, Ireland, 31 March, 1843. Hon. Colonel retired list Royal Canadian Artillery; Hon. Lieut. Col. retired list Royal Artillery; C. M. G. (1900); Hon. Sect. Canadian Patriotic Fund. (See "Who's who" and Debrett.) Came to Canada 1861 with 10th Brigade Royal Artillery; stationed at Halifax, Montreal, Kingston, and Quebec. Settled in Ottawa 1882 as Dominion Inspector of Artillery.

Married Quebec, April 25, 1867, Isabella, daughter of Robert

Hamilton [see Hamilton, of Hamwood, Quebec] and Isabella Thomson.
Issue:

> 1. Isabel Gladys Hamilton, born 2 August, 1884, married 1907 to Capt. Alan Z. Palmer of Ottawa.
> 2. Arthur De la Cherois, born 30 Oct., 1885, Lieut. R. O., Inspector Royal N. W. Mounted Police.
> 3. Robert Hamilton, born 28 Oct., 1887, B. Sc., Lieut. R. C. E.
> 4. William Eric Crommelin, born 24 Jan., 1890, B. Sc. Montreal.

Clubs: Rideau Golf, Rideau Curling, Gov. General's Curling, Matane Fishing, Denholm Fishing, Minto Skating.
Residences: 170 Cooper St., Ottawa, Ont. Carnagh House, Co. Armagh, Ireland.

Lineage.

William Irwin of the Irwins of Bonshaw, Scotland, had a son
William Irwin, who obtained in 1680 grant of Carnagh estate, Co. Armagh, Ireland. His grandson
William Irwin (1675-1737), landowner, married Sara Monson. Their son
Arthur Irwin (1725-1795), landowner and J. P., Greenmount, Co. Monahan, married Alicia, daughter of Daniel Kelly of Castle Dawson, Armagh; their 4th son James was great grandfather to President Benjamin Harrison, U. S. A.; their eldest son
William Irwin (1756-1835), born Greenmount, landowner and J. P., married Eliza (daughter of John Owens of Stonehouse, Co. Louth). His second son:
John Robert Irwin (1788-1871), born Greenmount, J. P., Lieut. H. M. 25th Foot (1809) of Carnagh House, married Elizabeth Emily (daughter of Nicholas De la Cherois Crommelin of Carrowdore Castle, Co. Down. Descended from a French family, who left France on the Revocation of the Edict of Nantes). Issue:

> 1. William Arthur (1841-96), married Eliza Browne.
> 2. De la Cherois Thomas (as above).
> 3. John Frederick (1847-1901), married Anne Stannistreet.
> 4. Fitzjohn Robert (1849-82), married Saidee Murray-Ker.
> 5. Edmund Herbert De Moleyns, born 1856, married Mary Boyer.
> 6. Emily Elizabeth, born 1850.
> 7. Alice Clara, born 1852.

Arms (Registered Ulster's office 1907): Argent on a fesse engrailed gules between three holly leaves vert, a trefoil slipped or. Crest: On a wreath of the colours a forearm vambraced charged with a trefoil as in the arms. The hand bare grasping a thistle all proper. Motto: "Nemo me impune lacessit." Pendant from the shield, the badge of the Most Distinguished Order of St. Michael and St. George.

Kerr of Toronto.

THE HON. JAMES KIRKPATRICK KERR (*), K. C., born Township of Puslinch, Ont., 1st Aug., 1841. Life Senator of Canada since 1903; called to Bar 1862; Q. C. for Ontario 1876, for Canada 1881; Grand Master of Masonic Lodge of Canada 1874-7,

created Knight Grand Cross of the Temple (England and Wales) 1883; Speaker of the Senate of Canada, 1909-11; summoned to His Majesty's Privy Council for Canada, 6th Oct., 1911.

Married (firstly) 1864 Anne Margaret (daughter of the Hon. William Hume Blake, Chancellor of Upper Canada). She died 1882 without issue. Married (secondly) 5th Dec., 1883, Adelaide Cecil, daughter and co-heir of the Rev. George Stanley-Pinhorne, Cumberland, England, and niece of the Rt. Hon. Alexander Staveley Hill, K. C., M. P. of Oxley Manor, Staffordshire. Issue:

1. Cecil Vivian, born 16 Nov., 1884; married, Toronto, 30th Sept., 1909, George Hamilton Cassels, Barrister of Toronto, 2nd son of Walter Gibson Pringle Cassels (q. v.), Judge of the Exchequer Court, Ottawa.

2. Nadine Jane Hamilton, born 31 Dec., 1885, married, Toronto, 16 Feb., 1909, Edmund Featherstone Osler (late of the Duke of Cambridge's Own Middlesex Regiment), Lakeview Farm, Bronte, Ont., 2nd son of Sir Edmund Osler, M. P. of Craigleigh, Toronto.

3. Evelyn Adela, born 9th March, 1887, married, Toronto, 3rd Sept., 1908, William Harty of Kingston, Ont., 2nd

son of the Hon. William Harty, Ex.-M. P. of Kingston.

4. Stanley Chandos Staveley, born 6 April, 1889; B. A.
   Toronto.
5. Florence Petronelle, born 25 Aug., 1893.

Clubs: Toronto, York, Toronto Hunt, Ontario Jockey, Ontario, and
Rideau (Ottawa).

Residence: Rathnelly, Toronto, Ont.

Lineage.

James Kirkpatrick Kerr (as above) is eldest son of

Robert Warren Kerr (1810-72), Co. Sligo, Ireland. Educated Trinity Coll., Dublin; came
to Canada 1832, settling in the Township of Puslinch, U. C., becoming City
Chamberlain of Hamilton, Ont. He married Jane Hamilton (daughter of James
Kirkpatrick of Wentworth Co., U. C.). His father

Robert Kerr, Esq., of Co. Sligo, married Mary, daughter of James Warren, Esq., of Sligo Co.

Arms : Quarterly: 1st and 4th vert on a chevron between in chief a fleur-de-lis and in base
a martlet argent three mullets gules, a crescent of the last in dexter chief for difference
(for Kerr); 2nd and 3rd azure the sun in splendor (for Lothian): over all an
escutcheon of pretence; party per pale gules and sable; on the fess point of a saltire
argent, between four hunting horns stringed and garnished of the last, a cross moline
vert (for Stanley-Pinhorne).

Crest : A stage's head erased vert, a crescent gules for difference. Motto: "Bon y bel
assez." Other quarterings : Staveley, Newton, Cowton and Chandos-Pole.

Kirkpatrick of Kingston

L T. COL. SIR GEORGE AIRY KIRKPATRICK, K. C. M. G.
(deceased) († ‡). born Kingston, Ont., 13 Sept., 1841; Lt. Col.
late 47th Frontenac Batt.; barrister 1865; Q. C. 1880; L. L. D. Trin.
Coll., Dublin; M. P.; Speaker of the House of Commons 1883-7; Member
P. C. of Canada 1891; Lt. Gov. of Ontario 1892; K. C. M. G. 1897.

Married (firstly), 1865, Frances Jane (daughter of the Hon. John
Macauley of Kington). She died 1877. Issue:

1. Col. George Macauley, born 1861. Inspector General of
   the Australian forces.
2. Arthur Thomas, born 1871. Barrister.
3. William Macpherson, born 1874. General Freight Agent
   C. P. R., Montreal.
4. Guy Hamilton, born 1875.
5. Helen Young.

Married (secondly), 1883, Isabel Louis (daughter of Hon. Sir David
Lewis Macpherson, K. C. M. G. of Ottawa). Issue:

Eric Reginald Macpherson, born 1884. (King's Own Yorkshire
Light Infantry.)

Sir George died Sept. 13, 1899,

Lineage.

Ivone Kirkpatrick (*temp.* David I of Scotland) had a grandson Ivone, who received in 1232 from King Alexander II a charter of Closeburn in Nithsdale, Dumfrieshire; his son

Adam, Lord of Closeburn, had a son

Stephen, Lord of Closeburn, whose son

Sir Roger Kirkpatrick was Justiciary of Galloway, Ireland, in 1304. His son

Sir Roger captured in 1355 the English castles, Durisdeer and Caerlaverock. Burke says of him: "Sir Roger was one of the first who stood up for the King, Robert the Bruce, as he was returning from striking Red John Cummin in the Dumfries Church. Sir Roger went into the church, exclaiming: 'I'll mak sicker [sure]' and then gave Cummin several stabs with a dagger." Hence the crest and motto. He was murdered by Sir James Linsay in 1357. His son

Winfred (Umfred) was one of the hostages for the payment of King David's ransom. His son

Roger married Margaret, daughter of Thomas, 1st Lord Somerville, and Janet, daughter of Sir Alexander Stewart of Derneley. Roger's 2nd son

Alexander was made Baron of Kirkmichael as a reward for the capture of James, Earl of Douglas, in 1484. Alexander's great grandson

William Kirkpatrick died 1686. His eldest son was

George of Knock, born 1671, whose 3rd son

Alexander, born 1714, of Drumcondra House, Co. Dublin, Ireland, founded the Irish branch. Alexander's 3rd son

Alexander (1749-1818), of Coolmine, Co. Dublin, Ireland, was High Sheriff of the city and county of Dublin in 1798. His 4th son

Thomas (1805-1870) came to Canada, settling at Kingston; Barrister Q. C., M. P. for Frontenac; married 1829 Helen (daughter of Alexander Fisher). Thomas's 4th son was

George Airy Kirkpatrick (as above).

Arms: Argent a saltire and a chief azure, on the last three cushions or.   Crest: A hand
  holding a dagger in pale distilling drops of blood proper.   Motto: "I mak sicker."
  Surrounding the shield, the circlet and pendant badge of a Knight Commander of the
  Most Distinguished Order of St. Michael and St. George.

Matheson of Kildonan.

THE MOST REV. SAMUEL PRITCHARD MATHESON,
D. D. (*) Archbishop of Rupert's Land and Primate of all
Canada. Born Kildonan, Man., 20 Sept., 1852. Graduate of St. John's
College, Winnipeg, in Theology, B. D., D. D.; L. L. D., Cambridge;
D.C. L., Durham; Warden of St. John's College; Chancellor of the University
of Manitoba; ordained Deacon 1875; Priest 1876; Canon St. John's
Cathedral 1882; Dean of Rupert's Land 1902; Archbishop of Rupert's
Land 1905; Primate 1909.

Married (firstly) 1879 Saraphine Marie Fortin, daughter of William
Fortin of Iberville, Que. She died 1894. Issue:

> 1. Godfrey Arthur, born 1881, clerk, San Francisco, Cal.
> 2. Adele Constance, born 1883.
> 3. Mortimer, born 1885 (deceased).
> 4. Maude Elizabeth, born 1888.

NEILSON OF NEILSONVILLE

5. Nora Evelyn, born 1891.

6. Edgar Hugh Ernest, born 1892.

Married (secondly), 1906, Alice E. Talbot of Winnipeg. Issue:

1. Margaret, born 1907.

2. Mary Pritchard, born 1909.

Societies: A. F. and A. M. Past Grand Master.

Residence: St. John's, Winnipeg.

Lineage.

Alexander Matheson of Kildonan, Scotland, had a son

John, born Kildonan, Scotland, 1814; married, Kildonan, Man., Catherine, daughter of John Pritchard of Kildonan, Man. Issue:

1. John Pritchard, married Anne, daughter of John Fraser of Kildonan.
2. Margaret, married George Sutherland of Kildonan.
3. Catherine, married Angus Fraser of Kildonan.
4. Annie (deceased).
5. Mary, married Francis Murray of Kildonan.
6. Alexander, married Catherine, daughter of John McArthur of Grassmere, Man.
7. Samuel Pritchard (as above).

Arms: Party per pale; Dexter, ermine a cross gules, on a chief a pastoral staff surmounted by an open book proper (for Rupert's Land); Sinster, argent two Lochaber axes in saltire heads to the chief, between a cock in chief and a rose in base (for Matheson).

Neilson of Neilsonville (Quebec)

COL. JOHN LOUIS HUBERT NEILSON (*), Seigneur of Hubert, born Quebec, 24 March, 1845. Physician; late of the Royal Canadian Artillery; First Director General and organizer of the Canadian Army medical services; holds General Service medal, and Campaign medal, Soudan 1884-5 and two clasps; Knight of the Order of Melusine; Associate of the Order of St. John of Jerusalem in England.

Married, Kingston, Nov. 16, 1888, Wilmot, daughter of J. Bramley Ridout of England, late Lt. Col. 26 Scottish Rifles, and Wilmot Beresford Hayter, his wife.

Clubs and Societies: Quebec Garrison Club; Military Institute, Whitehall, London, England; Quebec Literary and Historical Society (President).

Residences: Corsock, Neilsonville, Quebec, also on his Seigniory of Hubert.

Lineage.

John Neilsonne, descendent of John Mac Neil, Earl of Carrick, was declared, in 1436, with his wife Isabel Gordoun, proprietors of Castle Corsock in Kirkcudbright, Scotland. His descendant

38

John Neilsonne and his wife, Margaret Gordon re-built the Castle in 1588, which date appears cut in stone, with their impaled arms over the entrance. Their grandson

John Neilsonne, of Corsock, married Mary Maclellan, daughter of the last Earl of Kirkcudbright. She died Sept. 28, 1697. (Note: This John Neilsonne was the prototype of the "Martyr" in Sir Walter Scott's "Old Mortality," being one of the leaders among the Covenanters. He was defeated at Rallion Green, made prisoner, subjected to the torture of the "boot," Dec. 8, 1666, and hanged, Dec. 14, at the Cross in Edinboro. His body was buried in Greyfriars. His son

John Neilsonne, of Corsock, married Anna Gordon of Carlestoun. He died '706. His monument is in Kirkpatrick, Durham. His eldest son

Richard Neilson, manufacturer at Dundee, married Janet Ray. Their son

Robert Neilson married Christina, daughter of James Guthrie of Craigie. His son

William Neilson (1726-80), born Balmaghie, Laird and Landowner, married Isabella, daughter of William Brown, Laird of Nunton and Langlands. Died Buitle, Jan 19. Issue:

      1. William (1767-1859), unmarried.
      2. Samuel (1772-93), unmarried.
      3. John (below).
      4. Agnes, unmarried.

His 3rd son

(Hon.) John Neilson (1776-1848), born Dornald, Kirkcudbright; King's Printer; Legislator, etc., in Canada; married Marie Ursule (daughter and heir of Jacques Joseph Hubert and Pelagie de Rieutord, Co-Seigneur of Hubert, Quebec). He died Neilsonville, Quebec. She died 1866. Issue:

      1. Samuel (1798-1837), unmarried.
      2. Isabel (1800-73), unmarried.
      3. William (1805-95), married Margaret Cassin (ancestors of Cornelius Neilson and Dr. Walter Neilson of Milwaukee, Wis.)

4. Margaret (1808-94), unmarried.

5. John (below).

John Neilson (1821-85), born Corsock, Neilsonville, married Laura Caroline, daughter and heir of Capt. John Moorehead (and Margaret Du Berger) of the British Army, and A. A. G. on the Staff Quebec. Issue:

    1. John Louis Hubert (as above).

    2. Laura Janet (1847-83), unmarried.

    3. John Samuel (1850-82), unmarried.

    4. Norman de Rieutord, born 1853, married Alice de la Naudiere.

    5. William Augustus.

    6. Alfred, born 1858, married Flora LeMoine.

    7. Ida Isabel.

    8. Henry Ivan, born 1865, married Matilda Anne Green.

Arms (Quartering Hubert and Moorehead): Azure two hammers in saltire or, in the dexter flank a crescent, and in base a five pointed star argent. Crest: A demi-man issuing from a mural coronet, holding over his shoulder a hammer all proper. Motto: "His Regi Servitium." Decorations: Pendant from the escutcheon: (1) The badge of the Order of St. John of Jerusalem in England; (2) the badge of the ancient Order of Melusine in France and Austria.

Pellatt of Toronto

COL. SIR HENRY PELLATT, Kt., C. V. O., A. D. C. (* †), born Kingston, Ont., Jan. 16, 1859. Capitalist; educated U. C. College; entered service of E. B. Osler 1874; junior partner Pellatt & Pellatt,

1881; head of firm since 1891; Knighted in 1905; C. V. O. 1910; Hon. A. D. C. to H. R. H. Duke of Connaught 1911; President Society of Knights Bachelor of England; Governor of Grace Hospital, to which he presented the Surgery Wing; Hon. Treasurer Trinity University; a noted athlete; created a Mohawk Chief 1910, with name Tanauyuasara (Dawn of the Morning); Lieutenant Queen's Own Rifles 1880; promoted through intervening grades to Colonel 1907; holds Long Service Decoration; took the Regiment to England 1910 at his own expense, to participate in manoeuvers; on Military Staff at Coronation of King George V.

Married, Toronto, June 15, 1882, Mary, daughter and heir of John Dodgson of Cumberland, England. Issue:

Reginald, born June 30, 1885, Captain 2nd Queen's Own Rifles; married, Toronto, Oct. 14, 1908, Marjory Carlyle, daughter of James Black Perry.

Clubs: Albany, Toronto, York, Rideau (Ottawa).

Residence: 559 Sherbourne Street, Toronto.

Lineage.

Apsley Pellatt (1736-98) married Sara (daughter of Thomas Meriton); died Islington. His son

Apsley Pellatt (1763-1826) married Mary, daughter of Stephen Maberly. They had fifteen children, of whom the fifth was

Mill Pellatt (1795-1863), who married Maria Esther (daughter of Thomas Wilde). He died at New Cross, near London, England, leaving issue of ten children, of whom the eighth was

Henry Pellat (1830-1909), born at Glasgow, Scotland, and married to Emma Mary (daughter of Henry Burton Holland of Peterborough, Ont.—a son of Major Ralph Burton Holland of the 14th and 16th Dragoons). Issue:
1. Mary Kate, born 1855, married Lt. Col. Robert Baldwin Hamilton of Toronto.
2. Marion Maria, born 1856, married Henry Edmond Morphy.
3. Henry Mill (as above).
4. Emily Mountford, born 1862.
5. Frederick Mill, born 1870.
6. Mill, born 1873.

Arms: Argent two bars sable, the upper charged with a bezant (for Pellatt). In center an escutcheon of pretence argent on a pale, per pale, vert and sable cottised gules, two looped bugle-horns of the first (for Dodgson). Crest: A lion passant argent, guttee sable, in his dexter paw an acorn slipped vert fructed or. Motto: "Devant si je puis." His shield surrounded by the circle of the Royal Victorian Order with pendant badge.

Addenda

Dominion of Canada

Arms: Quarterly of the arms of the first four provinces to enter Confederation, viz., 1. Ontario; 2. Quebec; 3. Nova Scotia; 4. New Brunswick.

No crest, motto, nor supporters.

1

Province of Ontario

Arms: Vert, a sprig of three leaves of maple slipped or, on a chief argent the cross of St. George.

Crest: A bear passant sable.

Supporters: Dexter a moose, sinister a Canadian deer, all proper.

Motto: "Ut incepit fidelis sic permanet."

Province of Quebec

Arms: Or on a fesse gules, between two fleur-de-lis in chief azure, and a sprig of three leaves of maple slipped vert in base, a lion passant guardant or.

Province of Nova Scotia

Arms: Or, on a fesse wavy azure between three thistles proper, a salmon

naiant argent.

Province of New Brunswick

Arms: Or on waves a lymphad with oars in action proper, on a chief gules
a lion passant guardant or.

Province of Manitoba

Arms: Vert on a rock a buffalo statant proper, on a chief argent the cross of St. George.

Province of British Columbia

Arms: Argent three bars wavy azure, issuant from the base a demi-sun in
splendour proper, on a chief the Union device charged in the centre
point with an antique crown or. (The foregoing is by royal warrant, the
following were added by Order in Council dated 25th May, 1911,
for use in the Great Seal of the province.)

Crest: Upon an imperial crown proper a lion statant guardant imperially
crowned all or.

Supporters: Dexter a Wapiti stag proper, sinister a ram of the ovis Mon-
tana proper.

Motto: "Splendor sine occasu."

Province of Prince Edward Island

Arms: Argent on an island vert to the sinister an oak-tree fructed, to the dexter thereof three oak saplings, sprouting all proper, on a chief gules a lion passant guardant or.

Motto: "Parva sub ingenti"

Province of Alberta

Arms: Azure in front of a range of snow mountains proper a range of hills vert, in base a wheatfield surmounted by a prairie both also proper, on a chief argent a St. George's cross.

Province of Saskatchewan

Arms: Vert three garbs in fesse or, on a chief of the last a lion passant guardant gules.

CUILEAN UASAL

₥aj. Gen. James Wolfe, killed at Quebec in 1759

Arms: Per fesse, argent and azure, in chief on a mount vert in front of an

oak tree proper a wolf passant of the last; in base two salmon naiant

barways in pale of the third.   Crest: A stork, wings elevated sable.

Motto: "Cuilean Uasal."

Sieur de Levis, Duc de Ventadour, Viceroy of Canada

Arms: Quarterly: 1, and 4, or three chevronelles sable; 2, and 3, chequy or and gules.

Marquis de Vaudreuil, Governor of Canada, 1755.

Arms: Argent a lion rampant gules.

Louis Joseph, Marquis de Montcalm. French General,
killed, Quebec, 1759.

Arms: Quarterly: 1, and 4, azure three doves argent; 2, and 3, sable a
tower of the second.

Motto: "Mon innocence est ma fortresse.

Jean Baptiste LeMoine, Sieur de Bienville, born at Montreal in 1680; founded New Orleans, La.

Arms: Azure three roses argent, in chief gules a crescent of the second between two mullets or.   Crest: A wild man carrying a club over his shoulder.

Motto: "Deo et regi."

Robert Cavelier, Sieur de la Salle, discoverer of the Ohio River and founder of Louisiana.

Arms: Quarterly: 1, and 4, argent a bend azure between six lozenges gules; 2, and 3, argent a chevron gules between, in chief, two garbs sable, and in base a crescent azure.

Pierre du Gast de Lussault, Sieur de Monts,
Lieutenant General, Acadia.

Arms: Azure five bezants.

Louis de Buade, Comte de Frontenac,
Governor of New France, 1672=98.

Arms: Azure three griffins or.

Le Chevalier René de Coutley (Son of Albert de Coutley
of Riom in the Puy de Dome), Chancellor; Chief Justice
of Rheims, 1684. Ancestor of the Coutlec family
of Ayliner, P. Q.

Arms: Sable an unicorn's head, maned, crined, and horned or, between
three fleurs-de-lys of the last.

Crest: Out of a ducal coronet with two pearls, an unicorn's head, as in the
arms.   Supporters: Dexter a griffin gules, wings, beak, and claws
or;   Sinister, a wolf per fesse or and gules.

Motto: "Fortiter et fideliter."

19

Antoine de la Mothe Cadillac, founded Detroit, 1701.

Arms: Quarterly: 1, Azure, a lion rampant or; 2, barry of six, argent and gules; 3, azure, a pale or; 4, argent, a tree proper within a bordure gules.

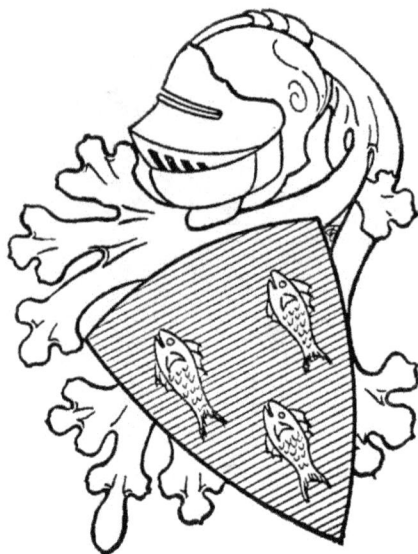

John Cabot and his son Sebastian, discoverers.

Arms : Azure, three chabots proper.

𝕸𝖆𝖗𝖖𝖚𝖎𝖘 𝖉𝖚 𝕼𝖚𝖊𝖘𝖓𝖊, 𝕲𝖔𝖛𝖊𝖗𝖓𝖔𝖗 𝖔𝖋 𝕮𝖆𝖓𝖆𝖉𝖆, 1752.

Arms: Argent a lion rampant sable armed and langued gules.

Crest: A lion issuant, as in the arms.

www.ingramcontent.com/pod-product-compliance
Lightning Source LLC
Chambersburg PA
CBHW070831100426
42813CB00003B/576